ANTARCTICA
A LONG-AWAITED
TRIP

Jane N. Hughes

Copyright © 2023 by Jane N. Hughes

All rights reserved. No part or portion of this book may be reproduced or used in any manner without prior written permission of the copyright owner except for the use of quotations in a book review as per the Australian Copyright Act 1968. For permission: janenhughes.com

Published by
Jane N. Hughes Melbourne, Victoria

ISBN: 978-0-6488978-6-6

Edited by Anne Schmitt & Dr. Christopher Ringrose
Cover photo by Jane N. Hughes
Cover design by Jane N. Hughes
Interior design by Jane N. Hughes

Disclaimer

This memoir reflects my own personal recollection of experiences through a successful trip to Antarctica in March 2023. The stories provide an outlook of this rare vacation and the views are not intended to hurt or harm anybody.

Antarctica: A Long-Awaited Trip

Jane N. Hughes

ANTARCTICA
A LONG-AWAITED
TRIP

JANE N. HUGHES

TRIP REVIVAL

Back in 2020, Robert and I had planned a trip to Antarctica to celebrate one of our big 'zero moment' birthdays. We are not party people and hence when my husband asked me what I wanted for the 'big five zero' I said Antarctica, not realising that he also wished to visit the place. After two years of planning, we left – but did not get there! Covid-19 shutdowns got to us in Ushuaia, Argentina, a day before the big trip itself. This account is a follow-up to my first book from 2020, that highlighted the experience of being in the wrong place at the wrong time due to Covid 19. That book, *Bad Timing: South America Mis(adventures) 2020* was published and still sells on many online outlets around the world. A link to purchase can also be found at www.janenhughes.com

This book focuses on the successful journey we eventually made and also gives tips and information which could be considered should you be planning a visit to Antarctica.

By 2023 we had waited three years for this time to come. "Patience is a virtue," they say. I never thought of myself as a patient person, but having brought up our children I knew that life has a way of shaping you, and therefore here I am.

The company which took us on our trip to Antarctica was exceptionally good at keeping their word honouring their promise since we paid them in 2019. We choose the *MV Ushuaia*, a small ship designed to carry eighty - four people, and we appreciated this intimate scale to our journey. We were able to land in every spot in Antarctica, since many locations impose an upper limit of one hundred people for landings. The ship was not luxurious in any way and could not provide a first-class cruising experience.

However, it exceeded our expectations of services and knowledge of Antarctica. *MV Ushuaia* was built in 1970, the same year I was born, and its main aim had been to undertake research in Antarctica. Eventually it became an expedition ship.

Leaving Melbourne

10th March 2023

Having had our excitement building for three years after Covid, we left Australia on the same date and month as in 2020. On this day 10th March 2023 we woke early as you often do when travelling, depending on the time of the flight. Our children came over to see us off and we were joined on the trip by two long-term friends. We got to the airport early enough and joined the queue at Qantas – not many airlines fly to South America from Australia so sometimes we had to suck it up. After twenty minutes a number of people who turned up late, but whose flights were boarding, were 'queue - jumped' by the staff.

We, on the other hand, had to wait for one-and-a-half hours. Where was the Aussie 'fair go' here? Service like this defeats the object of getting to the airport early. There was no apology, and the staff did not care one bit about those customers who turned up early.

I thought the service had gone down the 'shit creek'. (Oops did I swear? – not really, for I once saw a street in New Zealand with that name.)

After all the latecomers had been cleared it took us only five minutes and it was done. Our flight to Sydney was short and smooth. Breakfast was great, as was the service. We landed and transferred to the international terminal. Nobody likes the airports and particularly the security section, but this part of our world remains as crazy as ever. The security section was a 'united nations' workforce all from different background. It demonstrated the demographic of today's Australia. Caucassians were the minority. However, while everyone worked together, it was disorganised, chaotic, unfriendly, and rough. I hope not to use Sydney airport again, but never say never. The next wait commenced as we were directed to a gate, I had a snooze while Robert roamed around. Our friends were chilling in a business class lounge after upgrading. After a while, I figured out that people were not coming to the gate and Robert went to ask at the counter whether there was any issue. Well, they had changed our flight gate but had never announced it.

No wonder passengers end up being called on the loudspeaker for not turning up. Finally, we made our way to the revised gate, only to find that the flight was delayed by one and a half hours. We also received a general short SMS message from Qantas saying that we could claim our money back if we decided to call off the trip – were they serious? It had taken a lot of time to plan, save and arrange leave from work to enable this holiday to happen.

For Qantas to offer a refund was a bad joke, yet I remembered that during Covid they did not want to hear the word 'refund'. Finally, our plane turned up and we boarded. The pilot was great and explained the reason for the plane being late. You would be surprised by the explanation – there were no track vehicles available to push the aeroplane. What a joke for such a big international airport. I thought I lived in the First World and these problems could only occur in the developing world, as we continually get reminded. Our connecting flight from Santiago was only one hour after the scheduled arrival and one thing I have learnt over the years is not to stress when things are out of my control.

Before boarding the plane, I got in touch with our airport taxi lady in Buenos Aires to inform her that we were running late and that we would communicate with her while we got to Santiago. All good and organised – or so we thought. The in-flight attendants were all amazing; there was plenty of food and drinks. I even had an option of polenta (ugali in Kenya) and it was delicious. We were travelling with the international timeline and since South American time was behind Australian, we arrived on the same day we left Sydney.

We arrived in Santiago, Chile and our connecting flight had already left since we had been late leaving Sydney. The pilot had annouced that arrangement for another connecting direct flight were being made for us, so we had no stress...we thought. We were very wrong. We queued at Qantas help desk, where the two staff didn't seem to be in a hurry to serve us; another wait commenced. There were very few of us in line. One hour of waiting just went by like that. When our time came the guy got our passports and gave us a boarding ticket and a meal voucher on checking that the flight was due to leave soon.

We did not check the print on the boarding pass, but as we ran to the gate, I said to Robert that I could not see a Buenos Aires flight on the screen for our time. Still, we never gave the lack of our flight details on the screen any thought, but just kept on running like headless chickens. The thought of our flight leaving without us panicked us. We went through the gates without any issues and rushed to the plane. We boarded our flight, and I sat down next to a young man and began checking my phone. I asked him whether the flight was heading to Buenos Aires. "No," he said "to San Paulo in Brazil!" For God's sake, when would these dramas end? Thank God, the flight had not left the ground. I approached the steward; Robert had also picked up the issue and we both made our way to the entrance door. The pilot came out and said we had eight hours of detours before we got to Buenos Aires. However, we had no connecting flight from San Paulo to Buenos Aires. This was after doing fourteen hours from our original destination. We said no thank you. We opted to disembark, and he promised to have our bags removed from the plane.

Back to the drawing board. At the Qantas desk again, only this time there were no other passengers. The lady said the head office in Sydney had changed our ticket and put it through to San Paulo and it was a 'protected ticket'. I had no idea what this meant however the lady needed to get in touch with Sydney for help in booking the next direct flight.

Why Qantas put us through such hell and stress only God knows. Maria Theresa, the lady at the desk who was helping us, almost lost it on the phone with the Sydney staff. Qantas in Sydney were saying we had paid our original tickets through an Agency, and that we had to get in touch with them. Now, after 2020 we had vowed never again to book our tickets with an Agency since you get tossed around from one person to another. For that reason, I had purchsed our tickets directly from Qantas. After a long wait and a heated argument, we finally got our boarding passes for Buenos Aires! Hopefully our bags were going to be with us.

We reconnected with our friends, who had lost their phone on the plane and collected it from the information desk. At least this time we were on the same flight. Travelling is fun and English is barely spoken in this part of the world. Anyway, it was an adventure. Hopefully, there were happy times ahead. We arrived at Ezeiza airport in Argentina and 'surprise!' our bags were nowhere to be seen. We put in a claim and were in doubt about whether the bags would ever get there. Our host picked us up; she did not speak English; nor did we speak Spanish well, but I spoke very basic level and used an app at other times. One striking thing was that every driver used their mobile phones while driving. Valeria our taxi lady was continually texting when at the wheel. We thought one might win a medal for driving and texting at the same time, but here that was common with almost everyone.

We settled down into our accommodation with nothing to change into. I never thought I would use shampoo to both shower and wash innerwear and my top, but this time we had no choice. The weather was thirty-eight to forty degrees; no rain but the humidity was a killer; one could barely breath while outdoors. You would think we were in some sort of sauna, except that we had our clothes on.

BUENOS AIRES

11th March

I started to track the luggage on its journey from Sydney. No number to get in touch with, no email and we received auto-generated emails with no reply options. Great. In this modern time of communications, removing any direct human contact to deal with issues seems to be the best – for businesses. It has killed the concept of customer care and service. We did receive a WhatsApp messenger from Latam Airline, and they were trying to help even though they said they could not trace the luggage at all. I called our son back in Australia and asked him to track the luggage's trip from Sydney, and finally, the last place it was located was in Santiago.

Fingers crossed the bags were going to be united with us, since we were travelling onwards the following day. Finally, the bags were found but were given to a courier to drop them off. The courier allocated the drop-off time as between 1.00 and 4.00 p.m. Guess what? Nobody came during that allocated time; neither was there any communication about delivery. There was no number to call, contact or a Latam office anywhere in Argentina so I decided to go to the airport to try my luck in Latam queue. I found a good lady who promised the bags would be dropped off the same day. However, I was stressed not knowing whether or not we needed to cancel our next leg of travel.

After 7.00 p.m. I decided to cancel the next leg of our trip. I wrote an email to the airline since there was no other way of contacting them. Just as I pushed the 'send' button the courier delivered the bags. On checking them we could see they had travelled to San Paulo and then back to Ezeiza. The pilot had never removed them from his plane as promised. He could have been honest enough to tell the truth – that the flight had to be on time, and we would have known that our bags were going to San Paulo.

I also found out that taking the bags without the passengers being onboard was against aviation industry protocols. Maybe that part of the world operates differently or it just did not matter in this case. Relieved, my excitement at seeing the bags just made me scream and I felt like kissing the guy who dropped them off, but he had no life in him. The only thing I got was 'hola' and 'adios'. I signed off my bags and off he went. We were overjoyed by the fact that we were not going to have to go on dealing with the faceless customer 'service' chasing bags and jeopardising our Antarctica trip.

Robert and I went for a walk to celebrate our milestone then came back home, ate and relaxed, waiting what the next day might bring. It had to be better things than what we had gone through so far. The events which happened at the start of our travel were a reminder of the importance of being organised and giving yourself enough time to cater for any eventuality. We had a few days to play around with before the big excursion, and even though human beings can be anxious, this extra time provided us with a bit of reassurance.

OUR NEXT LEG

USHUAIA

After a couple of hectic days in Buenos Aires we were looking forward to the next leg of our journey – this time down in Ushuaia, since we were back on schedule with our holiday plan.
Our flight left in the morning, and we turned up at Ezeiza domestic airport where the queue was very long. However, it only took a few minutes for it to be cleared by the airline. It surprised me how quickly the queue moved. Our next step was security and even though I had travelled widely, this was the only place in my experience where police had handguns stuck in their pockets as they did a full search of the passengers. There were three female police and one male, one placed next to the queue and telling passengers in Spanish to remove anything in their pockets including electronics.

We managed to figure out the instructions. By the time we got to the conveyor belt we had everything on the tray ready to be scanned.
Once through the gate we got a full frisk check through the body, front and back. These policewomen were super-fast in their search. The flight was smooth with a snack on board. The view when floating down to land in Ushuaia was the most mesmerising thing you have ever seen. The place was beautiful – a little gem. Ushuaia resembled countries such as Switzerland or Austria where the Alps surround settlements and houses.

We went straight to our accommodation by taxi; Laguna Esmeralda was a bed and breakfast establishment. There is a lake that also goes by the name Laguna Esmeralda and that can be confusing as the taxi driver might think the destination is the lake itself, which is some distance from the accommodation. A misunderstanding would cost one a lot of money. Therefore, it is important to articulate the difference. Having been in this little town before, I could remember the place very well. The taxi driver seemed very interactive, though he did probably overcharge us. These things were out of our control and foreigners are often preyed upon.

We had first met the accommodation owner in 2020 when Covid was making everything crazy, Nancy looked after us during that difficult time and a friendship had developed. Over the three years, we had been communicating with and checking on each other, and when she saw us, it was like lost family members reuniting. She and her husband Daniel had made Argentinian lunch for us, so we all sat down together for the meal. He is a good cook. Nancy never spoke any English and we hadn't improved our Spanish since 2020 but with my broken Spanish and the use of the app we discussed Covid, business and life in general as it had affected us over the last three years. We then settled down in the same room we had in 2020.

13th March

We all relaxed, waiting for the time to set off for Antarctica. We had decided to get to Ushuaia five days before the big trip to cater for any other eventualities like delayed and cancelled flights and/or lost luggage. With all obstacles out of the way, we could now enjoy what Ushuaia had to offer. We reunited with our friends, who had got there one day before us. One of our friends decided to go hiking at Laguna Esmeralda Lake; I did this hike in 2020 and found it challenging but otherwise a great way to keep fit.

The walk took three hours round-trip, and the lake was just beautiful. But I had no desire to accompany her this time. The other three of us decided to visit the company (Antarpply) organising the tour to Antarctica. Everything seemed the same in Ushuaia apart from a few big new buildings – a sign that the small city was expanding. I hope it will not grow to be just another big city otherwise the uniqueness of this place will disappear. We walked to the office and met the same ladies who had been there in 2020 and it was great to catch up with them. One of the ladies bought my book online and she was wondering whether I was going to follow up this trip with another book. As a storyteller, I told her to keep an eye out as a pre-order was going to be organised soon.

The staff also told us the requirements we had to meet before we embarked on the ship; one of these was a covid negative result taken by ourselves, but we had to keep a photo of the result. While we thought all was clear for our big trip, we still had this nagging hurdle wondering if one of us might have turned positive. That would have been devastating. Otherwise, we had agreed the negative person would go ahead and leave the positive person back at the accommodation. How could one have forgiven Covid if the results of one of us turned positive at that crucial moment? It could have meant the three years were wasted and money lost, since the company was not offering a second round of compensation. All organised for the trip, we thought since we had a few days why couldn't we do the tour of the national park? We booked it for the next day and just like that another day was gone.

Tierra Del Fuego National Park

14th March 2023

The four tourists from Australia were ready to explore the End of the World National Park. The bus picked us up at 8.30 a.m. The day was rainy and very grey and hence our tour commenced with uncertainty regarding the weather. The journey didn't take long and within twenty minutes we were at the park. Ushuaia is off the bottom of mainland Argentina; to drive to the mainland you need to go through Chile. This can create visa complications for tourists who don't have Chile visas. Therefore, before travelling by road from Ushuaia to Chile check out with your government on border requirements so you do not get stuck at the border. Ushuaia was 'discovered' by' British missionaries in the early 1830s. Those British got everywhere! According to the tour guide, the Indigenous people were still living there and the Argentinian government was trying to provide incentives for more Argentinians to come and settle, but they did not seem interested.

It was not until the big IT and electronic companies gave anybody who wanted to go and settle there three times their salaries - and that's when Argentinians moved down. The town now has a population of approximately 81,000 and still produces electronic gadgets.

The national park was amazing – there were few wild animals, unlike my native land – but a lot of birds and rivers. As we drove from one location to another the weather changed and snow started to fall, which was an added delight and converted horrible bad weather into the excitment of playing with the snow. The mountains were all white and the views were just spectacular. It was hard to believe that we were at 'the end of the world'. We rode on the steam engine railway as part of the tour, and this train mimics one of the oldest trains used by prisoners in the early days of Ushuaia settlement. The trains were well-maintained, and this part of the tour was organised and well-coordinated. The steam and the noise coming from the train brought back good memories of when I was a little girl growing up in a small village in Kenya.

The atmosphere, the environment, and the services the staff offered were worth every coin used for this trip. The tour guide was well-informed, with a lot of knowledge at hand. She had also lived in Australia so her English was easy to understand.

Therefore, I would say that a visit to this national park is a must if you ever find yourself in this part of the world. You will not be disappointed. The afternoon was well spent as I learnt how to make Argentinian empanadas. They are like samosas but unique in their taste, and I was keen to make some when back home. Learning is a life-long journey, and even with my tour to Antarctica I learnt a cooking skill.

Nancy, our host, was very pleased to pass on these skills. At dinner time we decided to go out. During Covid time, and before everything was locked down, we had visited a restaurant called Bondegòn Fueguino. From our memory the food was great, the service top notch and the atmosphere was just right. We called to make a reservation, but they never accepted any reservation. What we needed to do was to turn up early and queue. It was cold and rainy. We turned up a bit early since we wanted a table for four but the place was not open.

So, the girls went window shopping while the boys went to the Hardrock Cafe for a beer. I had not seen a Hardrock Cafe for years – we had one in Nairobi in the early 90s but it closed down. It used to be a high-end restaurant with a European vibe.

We went back to the restaurant at 7.30 and the queue had started to build up. We were number three by the time it opened at 8.00 p.m. There was a very long queue which was the measure of the popularity of this restaurant and the food this place offered. Finally, we got in and had our meals…Ooh my! I do cook and a good cook can tell you when the food is tasty. The girls had lamb, orange and honey with mashed pumking and or roasted potatoes. As for the boys, one had pork and the other beef stew. Our plates were very full, but we finished the meal. The dessert was just as good. We were never rushed to finish our food and we took our time to enjoy it. We left at 10.00 p.m and people were still waiting in the queue. We walked home and rested.

15th March

The day was gloomy and we decided to take it slow. Nothing was organised or arranged for this day. Argentinians eat a lot of meat, and I mean a lot. The vegetables in the supermarkets were minimal and even eating out there were more variety of meat on the menu than vegetables. I am not sure how their metabolisms work, since there were not a lot of obese people apparent in this society; they are solid but not obese and most of them also looked healthy even with the amount of protein they consumed.

One of the intriguing things in Ushuaia was the use of a toilet. In this part of the world once you use the toilet you need to separate paper and what goes through. This is done in those old houses due to their piping system, as I was informed. Therefore, after opening my bowels I found it very difficult to wipe my bottom put the paper in the basket and have the rest flushed down the toilet. This was not something I was used to, and even the thought of doing it was not comprehensible.

However, as a nurse, the positive side of doing this was that if you lived in this part of the world, it would be easy to identify any issues with your bowels since you would see any changes. Who even thinks of checking their bowels apart from crazy nurses like myself? Later in the day, we walked around Ushuaia; the beauty of the ever-changing mountains was unbelievable.

Our photos could not do justice to what the naked eyes could see. Walking was also the day's exercise and finally we settled in, cooking a meal. I took the opportunity to teach Nancy how to make chapatis.

16ᵗʰ March

Another day of waiting, so we had time to kill. We slept in, since there were no plans in place. After breakfast, we decided to visit the airline office and see whether we could change our flight on our return to Buenos Aires to make it a bit earlier. The service was great, but we could not change the flight times, or if we did it was more like purchasing the airline itself, with the amount of money they were asking. Anyway, we left and wandered around, finding a small corner shop where we had a hot dog overlooking the docking bay.

Whilst walking, I decided to visit the cemetery, which was just around the corner in that part of the city. It was surrounded by a high wall but the gate stood open during the day to allow visitors in. Robert was not interested in the cemetery tour, so he took his walk elsewhere and we agreed on a meeting point for later. At the gate two Argentinians were manning the cemetery, although they never said anything to me, just sitting there chatting and telling their stories happily.

As I walked around, it surprised me that Argentinians leave caskets in above-surface stone mausoleums, and the photos of the dead are placed in front of the caskets. The entrance to these mausoleums were clear glass where visitors can read and view the photos of the dead. The cemetery consisted of the older and more recently-deceased people and the caskets were in all sorts of different sizes and types. This is a different concept from where I come from. There, when somebody dies, they are buried away from home and rarely do people go to visit the grave – only when there is another burial. At that time, one goes searching for where one's loved one is kept. This practice came into effect some twenty years ago.

When I was little, relatives would be buried within the compound, but this changed with over population. I am generalising, basing my observations on the part of the world I come from Kikuyu and comparing it with other areas that practise different rituals in relation to death. It was interesting to compare the Argentinian approach to death with the beliefs I had grown up with.

After my cemetery visit, we had a look at different restaurants offering seafood, since pre-booking was not an option. There were quite a few, most of them very expensive, but we spotted one whose prices seemed reasonable. I was eyeing a king prawn dish, and after locating the restaurant we had to turn up half an hour before the restaurant opened to queue and secure a table.

Walked back home and relaxed for a while, and it was time for dinner. The restaurant opened twenty minutes before the indicated time. We were disappointed as we needed to queue for forty minutes in the cold; therefore, we checked another restaurant but were not impressed with the menu. We went back to Avenida San Martin Street and found a restaurant offering meat barbecue on an open fire. Even though we were not feeling like BBQ meat we agreed to go there. Our choice turned out to be perfect, and the food was great. I had never eaten barbecued meat as tender and tasty as theirs. The next step was paying the bill; since it amounted to a lot of pesos due to inflation, we were worried that we did not have enough.

We sat there counting all those Argentinian pesos thinking we were short, but in the end, we managed to gather the money. I guess we could have used our cards, but we also needed to get rid of the pile of notes we had collected, before setting off to the Antarctica trip. This was our last day in Ushuaia before the big adventure.

Antarctica Voyage

17th March

Our big day was here, with us all ready to go, we called our taxi driver but he was not nearby. We looked for another taxi but there were none, so our only option was to walk to the harbour. We had to pull our bags while our friends managed to pack their luggage in seven-kilogram backpacks. It was about two kilometres to the harbour and time was not on our side. I got ahead of the team and reached the harbour earlier than the rest. No security check and nobody was asking anything, even though there was a security machine to scan luggage. The officers were happy scrolling their phones while passengers passed by to their ships. I went straight to the *MV Ushuaia* and checked in. After clearance, I reached to our cabin to find my bags were already there. That's what I call service. My team members arrived and we met up at the bar, which consisted of different kinds of couches and loungers.

It would also be used as a lecture room. We met people from different countries and all sorts of lifestyles and got to know each other. Later *MV Ushuaia* held an introductory session where policies and emergency drills to protect people and wild animals were outlined. The drill part was interesting since we had to practise what we had learnt in case of emergency. While going through all the training and familiarising myself with the policies, I realised that we would be all alone in the wilderness and in the event of any emergency there would be nobody in sight to help us apart from ourselves. If any emergency occurred that could not be addressed on the ship, we would have to sail back to Ushuaia for support.

It was, therefore, important to ensure that everybody took great care of themselves and to thus minimised risks which could have jeopardised this long-awaited trip. It was also at this time that I began to hope that the One from above would exercise his powers to ensure that the whole trip did not have any further interruptions. Repatriation from the sea would have been difficult and even with good insurance coverage, it would be painful for everyone on the ship to sail back to Ushuaia.

With this possibility at the back of everyone's mind, it was fortunate that the passenger list was made up of sensible people. Even though accidents are sometimes hard to prevent, everybody did their part in ensuring that safety was key. After we got to know each other, we attended dinner – a three-course meal well cooked and tasty – before going to our rooms. I had a shower, aware that we were about to experience the Drake Passage, which promised to be very harsh, and settled into bed. At 3.00 a.m. the ship began to rock from side to side. People had been encouraged to take sea sickness tablets half an hour before the rocking commenced.

From this point, taking a shower was prohibited until we were in Antarctica. The rocking of the ship continued the whole night. I reflected that when babies are very young, we tend to soothe them by rocking them. But if rocking felt like this, no wonder babies stop crying! It's definitely not a good feeling. My head felt heavy, probably from the tablet I'd taken, and it was impossible to sleep well due to the repeated movements of the ship from one side to the other.

18th March

The dining room opened for breakfast at exactly 8.00 a.m., and closed at 9.00 a.m.; lunch and dinner followed the same on-hour sequence. In this situation, one had to be on time if one wanted food; and I realised that people could be very disciplined if time restrictions were enforced, since nobody was late and missed out on a meal.

Breakfast was served and the team was always on time. It was an English buffet and we had to queue for it. With the ship still rocking, it was a challenge to get hold of food. It seemed all too easy for the crew members, who walked as if they were leaning towards the side the ship was rocking yet could still do their job appropriately. As instructed by the head chef, one hand was for the food and the other for the ship, so that we could use that hold on to the rails. Trying to balance food and drinks on one hand while holding on to the rails with the other was like a puzzle and proved difficult.

On this particular morning a lot of people never arrived for breakfast due to the rocking of the ship; sickness had taken its toll on them and they were stuck in their rooms. The rocking never stopped, the whole day and night. One's body was however getting used to this movement and even though it did not feel right, survival was important.

There was an education session at 10.00 a.m. about the birds of Antarctica. Albatrosses and petrels are the most common birds found in the Southern Ocean and we could see them following the ship. They would fly for a while, then come down to the ocean and up again. It was interesting to watch how these birds behaved. They have a long history of following ships, ever since exploration and expedition times in the belief that the ship might be a source of food for them. Their age of sexual maturity is from five to fifteen years and they stay at sea all these years until they go to the land for breeding. Breeding occurs once a year, apart from the big Albatross, which nests twice per annum. They have a long lifespan of some sixty years. The wandering albatross has the largest wingspan of any bird measuring 3.5 meters. I never knew that birds could live so long.

They feed on squid, fish, penguins and octopuses. Every year many of these birds are killed by fishing lines, and there are concerns about possible extinction unless conservation is prioritised. I had little interest in birds as a rule, but this encounter with albatrosses and petrels was fascinating; getting an education about them provided me with an idea of the nature of their existence. After lunch there was another lecture – this one on the ice. I never knew that there were two types of ice – continental and sea ice. Continental ice is made up of large ice sheets formed from masses of glacial ice and are found on the ground and mountainous areas compressed over many years of ice formation.

It comes in all sorts of shapes and colours depending on the ice crystals, rock, dirt and algae. However, sea ice is found after seawater freezes and forms ice in the ocean. It was good to have taken this trip since I thought that ice was just ice, and that was it. We were also given information on icebergs and how they form. These icebergs and other features presented beautiful shapes and colours.

In shades of blue, green and brown. Cameras cannot do justice to the beauty Antarctica has to offer. The afternoon was free, so I had a sleep since my head was still heavy and I had felt dopy the whole day through.

Livingston Island

19th March

The waves had subsided somewhat and the rocking of the ship was not as severe as it was the day before. The captain woke us up with a nice Spanish song which played on the public audio system at 6.30 a.m. Then he made announcements in both Spanish and English. His deep voice was something that might have woken a baby up from sleep, and his first speech was to analyse the weather and what was expected of the day.

This being our second day on the ship, we were still on the journey to Antarctica and even though there were some activities on board, the anticipation of wanting to land in Antarctica was very intense. After breakfast, there was another educational presentation – this time on the Antarctica Treaty. Twelve different countries have claims on Antarctica and the first treaty was done in 1959 with the aim of promoting peace, and forbidding the establishment of military installations or nuclear plants. The main purpose of the treaty was to protect Antarctica's flora and fauna, wildlife, and the area is designated for research purposes only.

Thereafter in 1991, The International Association of Antarctica Tour Operators (IAATO) became the governing body for overseeing the tour operators, and governing the adherence to the listed rules and regulations designed to protect Antarctica. This body was created due to many organisations showing interest in visiting the continent; it was in the interest of everybody concerned to ensure that Antarctica is not ruined by human activities, destruction of the environment or killing of animals. Most tour companies which operate in Antarctica are members of IAATO. The continent is also the world's driest, and even though it snows there is minimal rainfall due to the harsh weather. Its vegetation takes forever to grow.

Our first evening outing was scheduled for this day and the weather was perfect for it. We were divided into eight different groups since there were eight boats (Zodiacs) for transport. I get hypothermia very quickly and you might think Antarctica would be the last place for me to visit due to this. However, we put on several layers of clothing before we stepped out of the ship. Once ready, we met at the deck and queued up in a group of eight. Our first step was to disinfect our boots in preparation for landing at the penguin territories, to ensure that we did not introduce anything detrimental into the pristine habitat of penguins. The same sanitisation was repeated when we got back from the landings.

We landed on Livingston Island and felt good to be out of the ship. I only saw small penguins in Australia in real life and watched *Happy Feet* the movie – but in reality, this was a very big colony. There were so many penguins walking around and they did not seem to have a pattern. Between the water and the land, there was also a family of elephant seals. They were massive animals, with their young ones, and once in a while, the parents would attack each other and then settle down.

Some leopard seals just lay on the rocks. In fact, they resembled the rocks, so it was very difficult to differentiate the animals from their surroundings. The seals did not seem bothered by human presence even though we were advised to walk in a group since if we were alone the animals would have thought we were prey. I was not sure when they hunted since they seemed very lazy and did nothing much to move around. It would have been interesting to watch them hunt but this never happened. The serenity of the place was seriously breathtaking. It seemed that everyone was excited, since the dining room later was very noisy, and people were animated, telling their evening outing stories. There was a bit of celebration with alcohol before we retired to bed waiting for the next day to offer another exciting trip out on to the land.

Hydrurga Rocks and Cuverville Island

20th March

The morning music came on – our sign to get up. The captain's deep voice in the public announcement welcomed us to another day in paradise. It was a paradise due to its beauty, and its serenity was pure. The captain outlined the day's weather and always reminded people to be extra careful out in the world. Breakfast was served earlier than usual and the day was scheduled with lots of activities. The ship was not carrying a lot of people so these were easy to organise. With few people on the ship, it was very easy to make connections and we became like a family. First, we visted Hydrurga Rocks, with which the crew was very familiar. The Rocks are a couple of small islands located in the Palmer Archipelago and being there gave us the feeling of Antarctica surrounding us.

The Rocks are home to Chistrap Penguins and there was a bit of climbing involved to reach the penguin colonies. It was also slippery on the ground and therefore extra care in walking was important to avoid falls and fractures. On arrival, we discovered an environment of big brown rocks. As we walked, we passed a Weddell seal that looked exactly like the rocks; it had similar markings and spots and was almost as immobile. It would have been very easy to make a mistake and step on it. The guide was standing not far from the seal and directed people to the path around it. Further on, more seals were lying idle with their young ones not very far off and like any young creatures, the young seals were having a great time playing with each other.

The seals and the penguins coexist, and proximity did not seem to cause any issues. Like every creature or animal, seals can be aggressive if approached and therefore one had to give them some distance and not disturb them. Any animal will protect their territory or their young if they think their lives are in danger. Within the scenery, the plain (black and white) penguins were numerous, making up another colony. I stood there looking at how well they walked on those rocks and realised that they studied their surrounding first before using the easiest way to enable them to move – just like humans.

In between the rocks, the penguins would check on the trenches and measure the depth then proceed with their walk if they felt safe. They are very analytical in their assessment of the surrounding environment. Where the snow was involved and hilly, the penguins would walk to a point and, once tired, would slide off the snow. I guess they walked smart, based on my observations. Penguins never seem to be bothered by the presence of humans – they even came closer to people and maybe were curious about what these different species could be.

While they approached people, it was a rule of the visit not to touch them, and to let them be; we were also warned to keep away from their walking paths. This was to ensure that no diseases were introduced to the penguins by humans. The trip was a great success, so wonderful; having experienced the view of these animals we went back for lunch, before the next landing. Lunch was served, and we had a bit of a break and nap before the next excursion, scheduled for the late afternoon: to Cuverville Island which consisted of a hill divided into two parts with a middle point. On landing, we had a choice of which side to walk on. I started off to my right and soon discovered another colony of penguins.

Gentoo Penguins were the ones found here, and there were many. The penguins were swimming or feeding their young ones, and hundreds were standing on the hill. They walked freely, taking care to watch where they stepped and making a lot of noise. The weather was beautiful with the sun beaming high it wasn't cold. Our Zodiac came to take us back to the ship and the driver decided to manoeuvre around different icebergs. At one iceberg a leopard seal was sleeping comfortably as if it had not a care in the world. That was a bonus to see and we took a few photos. Back at the ship, we had dinner, listened to announcements concerning the next day, and tried a salsa dancing class.

We went to sleep satisfied with the day and waiting for the next day's excursions, which were normally dictated by the weather.

Paradise Bay and Antarctica 21st March

Our group was very lucky, in that the weather was favourable, and we could not ask for anything more. The head of the crew members mentioned that we were a most fortunate group, since the weather had been terrible a few weeks before. I guess that, knowing we had been waiting for three years, the One Above must have listened to our prayers and guaranteed good weather as a way of rewarding our patience! The weather could be very unpredictable, and we lived in the hope that it would enable us to continue enjoying our time in Antarctica. Early breakfast was now the norm, and on this day, we had two trips organised, one in the morning and the other in the late afternoon. The first excursion consisted of an hour with the Zodiac in Paradise Bay based on the western Antarctica peninsula. The group was divided into sets of six people to provide us with an amazing experience and space to take photographs.

We were in the second group and dressed for the weather; even though it was sunny it was not hot outside. I had to put on three layers of tops, trousers, and gloves as well as four sets of socks, two thermals and two t-shirts. One of the things which worried me was getting cold and not being able to enjoy myself. Therefore, while others might have dressed differently, I had to ensure that I was well covered up to avoid becoming a problem to the rest of the Zodiac team expeditioners. While waiting for our group to get picked up, we had an opportunity to see whales, which had visited the sea near the ship. There was a family of three, a father, a mother, and a baby. The mother was nursing the baby and so they were both very playful.

It was a sudden surprise – something we had not expected but worth every click of our cameras. Our trip to Paradise Bay went smoothly and it really surprised me how surreal this paradise appeared: a very calm area with glaciers all over the place, some of them blue. It is very difficult to compare the nature of this amazing place since there is nothing in my experience to do it with. The little icebergs, each with their different shapes, in the middle of nowhere, were unbelievable.

If this was not paradise, then I was not sure what else could be viewed as one. The penguins were always swimming, and now and again a bunch of them swam near people. The only problem with the penguins swimming was our inability to take any quality photographs. They were so fast and tiny that it was difficult to capture their images.

Our excursion was extended to the mainland of Antarctica, and we landed at the place that we had dreamt of feeling our presence. It was all snow; the beauty of the mountainous snow, and the feelings it aroused, were exciting. We took photographs and hike a little, bit while we satisfied our egos - our sense of having been to Antarctica! We felt very privileged. There was no seawater or anything else visible - just snow - and glad that the peninsula stop on our way to Antarctica had provided us with the opportunity to explore and see animals and the different shapes of icebergs and mountains. Otherwise, there is nothing to register on mainland Antarctica apart from a good feeling of having visited this great place in the world. We had our lunch and an afternoon rest before our afternoon tour.

I never thought that we could hike in the snow but that was the agenda that afternoon. The layers of clothing I had worn against the cold were now making my life unbearable. Hiking proved challenging due to the heat generated by my body. It was steep and difficult in the snow, and quite challenging for some. The crew said they had never ventured so far up this hill; it was the first time the weather had permitted such a hike.

We came to another penguin colony; I had never realised that they could climb so high up in the snow. Like people they would get tired, so they would use their fins to climb up, and slide on their bellies on the snow while coming downhill. I also realised that they were eating something from the snow, and wondered what that could be, since there was no obvious nourishment there. Observing more closely, I discovered that they were indeed eating the snow itself. Out of curiosity, I wanted to know more about penguins consumption of snow, and the answer was in order to hydrate and cool themselves. While the penguins were busy interacting with nature, the smell of their faeces was hard to miss! Penguins also played with their young and it was interesting to see how they fed. A mother is always a mother; as soon as the young penguins nagged their mother for food they just jumped into water and swam away to get some.

Since the chicks could not swim, they were left standing there wondering what else they could do. (I guess this was a punishment from the parents for asking for too much). The traits of these birds enabled me to realise that they are just like humans – the only thing they could not do was to communicate with us. The evening concluded with a tasty dinner and debriefing. There was an education session on Argentinian drinks and for this evening they focussed on their whiskey called The Smuggler.

The Smuggler was first bottled in 1835 and derived its name from the smugglers who traded around the Scottish islands. After this lecture on The Smuggler, we were offered a few bottles to have a taste of this old Argentinian whiskey. I am not a whiskey fun, and I rarely drank it before: but, on this day, I had three shots and it tasted very smooth. However, my whiskey experience (which is zero) meant that it might actually have been horrible, but I enjoyed it nonetheless. Certainly, a lot of people kept going back for more. This was either an indication that it was good, or that people could not afford to buy another type of drink. There was a bit of music at the bar and people were dancing and celebrating another successful day in Antarctica. Finally, we retired to bed hoping the next day was going to be as successful.

Petermann Island

22nd March

Another day, another fun time – we hoped. The ship was calm and there was snow everywhere upon it. We were stationary and the engine was less noisy. The scenery outside was beautiful: no rain, but snowy, which made the moment very refreshing. The itinerary was set out every night and we knew that this day we were to visit Petermann Island. An early announcement came on the PA, the captain mentioning that while the weather did not look favourable, we could still try to go out. He also articulated clearly that safety was his number one priority, and that people should be extra careful while out on the landing. I was not going to complain since we had a few good days; if this one turned out to be unpleasant, we could cope with it. We had breakfast and headed off to Petermann Island, located off the northwest coast of Kyiv Peninsula.

This island is known to support breeding colonies of some three thousand pairs of gentoo penguins. Adélie penguins, Wilson's storm petrels, imperial shags and south polar skuas also nest on this island in small numbers. However, during our visit, we saw few other birds, but there were plenty of penguin colonies. There is a saying 'seen one, seen them all'. but this was not the case with penguins. They are just adorable creatures, and you can spend ages watching their behaviour. On this day, the penguins were hiding behind the rocks to protect themselves from the extreme weather – cold with a bit of wind. For us, it was unbearable, and I imagined if the penguins themselves felt cold, humans had no chance of surviving that environment.

The chicks were playing around, and the fur seals just lay on their rocks doing nothing. The weather became very harsh and not conducive for any outside activity, so we had to go back to the ship. We had to hurry as if an emergency had occurred, since things can turn nasty very quickly in Antarctica. The afternoon was spent catching up with other expeditioners and crew members. People played cards and caught up by telling stories from their various countries.

Otherwise, we also had some time to ourselves, and it seemed the day's excursions and exploring outside were finished like that. Due to the extreme weather and the anticipated storms the captain decided to take the journey back to the mainland using a long route to avoid the storms which could have been dangerous to us all. The ship was rocking everywhere and sleeping became a nightmare. We hung in there till morning.

Deception Island

23rd March

The outside activities had been completed, and now the main priority was to get back to Ushuaia safely. The captain informed us that the trip was going to be long since he was going around the storm; therefore, it was going to take an extra day to get to Ushuaia – hence his decision to leave early. We felt short- changed, having missed one full day in which we could have explored Antarctica further; but our health and safety came first. The waves in the sea were as high as eight metres and the ship was rocking more than ever. As the ship rocked from one side to the other, more people felt sick – including myself. I forgot to take my tablet on the way back and was 'as sick as a dog'. I cannot recall when I ever felt that sick. After that, I took tablets every day to avoid sea sickness.

This is one thing travellers never talk much about – the Drake Passage is one of the most dangerous sea lanes in the world and it can make for a harsh and bumpy journey.

The early morning call informed people that we were almost at the entrance to Deception Island, and that anyone interested in viewing was welcome. We had to wake up and get to the deck to avoid missing anything exciting. The weather was windy and harsh, and even though I managed to get outside, I lasted less than five minutes. The Island is an active volcano based in the South Shetland Islands close to the Antarctic Peninsula. It has a horse-shoe shape, and it is surrounded by barren volcano slopes, steaming beaches and ash-layered glaciers. The narrow Neptune's Bellows provide a sheltered harbour, but also form a narrow entrance. I had my camera and a phone, and I wanted to capture good photos from both gadgets. I also had gloves, since the weather was not that friendly, but the moment I removed the gloves my fingers got cold and numb. So, I was forced to get back into the ship and look out from the bridge. Ofcourse, the photos here were not as clear as the ones taken from outside.

The passage to the island was very narrow, but the captain used his experience as he expertly manoeuvred the ship into the harbour. The view of brown and snowy hills was beautiful. The captain went around the harbour twice to give people enough time to take photos and view the scenery. There was volcanic soil in some parts, mostly near the mountains, and this was our last sight of mountains or scenery. The rest of the day was spent enjoying the rocking ship and our long journey back to Ushuaia.

Stuck Inside MV USHUAIA 24th and 25th March

These days were spent on the ship. Nothing much was happening; there was one education session on Antarctica, followed by the *Happy Feet* movie in the afternoon. The waves were so high, and the ship rocked so much, that most people were stuck in their cabins. Even though the rooms were comfortable, it was a long day living in a confined space and not being able to do anything, due to the instability on the ship.

Therefore, I took the time to download my photos from the camera to the laptop, just to be safe. I am passionate about good photos but am also aware that I take them for my own satisfaction, since nobody will ever watch them again after I have shown them to friends and family members. The photos are normally stuck in the computer; one is printed as a reminder, and the rest become history.

The afternoon then became very exciting and competitive as activities were organised with quizzes from Antarctica. There were six groups competing on the knowledge of Antarctica that we had gathered over our trip. Our group comprised both Spanish and English-speaking people and there was a lot of energy within the group. Trying to read the questions in both languages within a limited time was exciting.

The team leader held the question paper while everyone surrounded her and tried to read in whatever language suited them in the limited time available, in order to make an instant answer. I thought it was hilarious, even though our target was to get the questions right for the competition. Even with the combination of people speaking two different languages, the teamwork was great, and we came second overall, beating other single language groups.

That same afternoon, we had a final briefing for our final night and to prepare for disembarking. One interesting thing was that *MV Ushuaia* had prepared a usb that was gifted to all the passengers, with all the information and photographs for our trip. The information was put in either English or Spanish, depending on the passengers. We had dinner and there was no debriefing. All the captain wanted to do was to get his passengers safely back on shore. The sea was still rough that night but somehow, we managed to sleep.

SAYING GOODBYE

26th March

This was our final breakfast before disembarking. Over the week everyone had got to meet new people with the same interests and become friends. We had also built a rapport with the expedition staff members. It was sad to part ways after being on a ship and lonely continent together for ten days. Nothing lasts forever and we exchanged contacts, photos to remember each other by, and shared memories before it was time to get off the ship as the final step of a great trip. On this day everyone was waiting a bit earlier than usual for the dining room to be opened. Once breakfast was served people got to interact for the last time. It did not take long for the crew to announce that it was safe to disembark. We went back to our cabins to collect our belongings and, just like that, the trip was over. So, after all the disappointments, anticipation, and waiting for three years to travel on that cruise to Antarctica, it proved to be the best thing ever. We felt a little flat after the trip.

After years of anticipation and having fulfilled a lifetime dream, there was no more waiting anymore. But we were fully satisfied with our experience of Antarctica and its beauty.

We are now advocates for keeping that continent free from human interruption/disruption, or pollution, whether economic or otherise.

Important Points

Visiting Antarctica is maybe one of the most challenging things you can do, but also one of the best thing you can do. This is due to the length of time taken to travel to that continent, and going through the Drake Passage can be extremely challenging. Passing through the Drake is one big thing which never seems to be talked about, and I am not writing about it here to scare anybody off. Just be aware that it is a rough journey through heavy seas. It can also be unpredictable and dangerous. To provide a little bit of comfort on this stage of the journey, taking the sea sickness tablets well before hitting the Drake would be ideal. The rocking can be uncomfortable, but one can handle it better if not sick. Taking something to entertain yourself is also paramount. There is no free internet and the one available on the ship is expensive. Prepare your own entertainment, because the lectures and activities provided on the ship are not enough to keep you occupied through the days of the voyage.

Even with good insurance cover while travelling to Antarctica, you would never want to fall sick out there. The main hospitals are based on the mainland and by the time the repatriation team gets down to you, your life could be lost. Your only sources of immediate help are the ship's crew and the people touring with you. It is therefore important to ensure that before visiting Antarctica, prospective travellers get a health clearance from their medical team.

Hopefully, this ensures that you can survive without any issues out in the sea and in the middle of nowhere. Where chronic diseases cannot be managed appropriately, it is better to watch documentaries in your own comfort zone rather than take the risk. Otherwise, all being well and if you are fit for travel, then you will fall in love with Antarctica. Following instructions from the crew members is important, as these people have been doing these tours for years. Their knowledge on the environment cannot be underestimated. Look, learn and listen to be a good expeditioner. Avoid putting yourself at risk to get that perfect photograph, and remember that there is no perfect photograph except in the eye of the beholder.

While social media has uplifted people in one way or another, do not put yourself in a dangerous position to impress the world. You would never want to trend for the wrong reason.

Back on the Mainland

After we left the ship, it was still early, and the weather was cold and miserable. We tried to kill some time by walking slowly back to our former accommodation. Nancy was happy to see us and have us hang around until the flight time for Buenos Aires. After warming up we walked to downtown Ushuaia, but there was nothing much happening on a Sunday. We ate lunch, said our goodbyes, and left for the airport. We might never see Nancy again but her positive attitude with her business will see it thrive. Our hostess in Buenos Aires picked us up from the airport and we headed straight to her bed and breakfast. We shared some great moments since she was interested in our Antarctica trip. We had a cup of tea and viewed some photos and videos. Our next plan was to visit the celebrated Iguazu Falls.

Since we were in Argentina why not visit this magnificent place? However, our flight from Iguazu was landing at Jorge Norman airport and we were struggling to work out how much taxis cost. As we were ripped off during our last visit. Valaria offered to come and pick us up and I could not believe it since it was forty minutes away and the traffic could be terrible. What a nice person! We went to bed and looked forward to our next excursion.

IGUAZU FALLS

Brazillian Side

With the Antarctica trip behind us, we could now enjoy the last few days to recover and visit Iguazu. Our flight was early so by 4.00 a.m. we were up and off to the airport and landed in Iguazu without any hiccups. We had not organised transport and therefore we were relying on public transport. As planned, we wanted to visit Iguazu Falls from the Brazilian side first; and when the bus turned up, we thought we had explained what we required. With the help of a guy from Costa Rica who spoke some English, we were set. Halfway there the bus stopped on the side of the road, and the driver said we needed to change buses for the Brazilian side. All was good until we arrived only to be told that we were on the Argentinian side. The Costa Rican alighted and did not seem to care. However, the coordinator of the bus was great; he talked to his driver and instructed him to show us where to board the bus for Brazil. We went back to the bus stop and off to Iguazu bus terminal and enquired about the tickets.

The guy at the counter did not seem to care but nevertheless provided us with the tickets and directed us to the boarding platform. Planning for any eventuality during a holiday is important – since we had plenty of time, we were not concerned about any unforeseen issues. These spontaneous travel arrangements made the trip interesting, and we learnt as we went. With our history of having issues here and there we decided to allocate a few days or hours flexibility, to remove the stress associated with the travel shortfalls. The bus stopped at the border between Argentina and Brazil; we all got out at that point, and there was no demarcation as such. We presented our passports to immigration; unfortunately, there is no stamping of passports anymore, so there is nothing to show that I visited Brazil, apart from the memory I hold.

The migration officers also used pen and paper to write our details down, despite the fact that they had computers in front of them. Nobody seemed to use them in either Argentina or Brazil. On the bus the driver decided to give his passengers information about the trip and did so in Spanish; it took forever to understand what he was saying. I could only pick up one word here and there. After he finished, we were left in the dark, not knowing what was happening.

I told the bus driver that we had no idea what he had just told his passengers, and asked whether there was anybody on the bus who spoke a bit of English so they could briefly explain to us. One lady and her son spoke a bit of English and informed us the driver was talking about the bird park and the falls; he was suggesting how many hours one should spend on the bird park. It sounded like a lot more information when delivered in Spanish!

On the Brazilian side of the border, they preferred to either use Argentinian pesos or American dollars, since their reel (the local currency) was very low. Not that the Argentinian peso was much better. Big road projects were being constructed, and there were ugly-looking billboards advertising all sorts of things along the route. There were also a lot of hotels along the road to the national park, but one thing I thought did not fit in was a massive hotel just next to the park. This was in contrast with the Argentinian side, where hotels were set away from the park. We had paid for the park online but on arrival, we found that the bird park fees were not included. The bird park was a separate package of thirty-two dollars for two. Since time was on our side, we paid to visit the bird park first before the falls.

This part was very well organised with a variety of birds, snakes, and butterflies. The park was in real forest bush and the coolness and atmosphere were relaxing, particularly since it was generally very hot and humid.

This environment provided us with a perfect time to cool down. We spent a good two hours walking around, reading, and watching different species of birds. The park also had a few cafes and we sat down in one for lunch and some drinks. I had never drunk a refreshing orange juice straight from fresh oranges as we did in this restaurant. Our next step was Iguazu Falls, so we presented our tickets and boarded a double-decker bus. It was a smooth ride, and the only downside was the pre-recorded lady who spoke in broken English; we could barely understand what she was trying to say. She sounded like me when I tried to speak Spanish, and not many people would give me a listening ear. We commenced our walking trail. It took us one and a half hours to make our way, viewing how amazing the falls looked from different locations and walking towards the largest part of the falls. It was quite a distance and as we got closer the sound of the falls became stronger and louder.

Never in my whole life could I have thought that something like that could exist. We took our photos and selfies for memories and shared some with friends and relatives online who 'travelled with us'. Yes, it is hard to believe, but some friends take the trip with you – they follow you around, and you feed back to them through social media. We had to go back to Argentina for our accommodation since we had not yet checked in. I must say that the owner of Posada Enki where I had booked our accommodation was extremely helpful in providing information on where to get buses and the amount to pay; which was helpful since, as in all tourist destinations, tourists are often ripped off.

I got in touch with him to know the best hotel we could dine in after a long day walking on the trails of Iguazu Falls. His recommendation did not disappoint us, and we had dinner at Restuarante La Rueda. The food and service there were so good it made us forget how tired we were. At the end of the evening, we needed a taxi to Posada Enki, but the first taxi we called was asking for too much and would not budge on the price. I called our accommodation host who organised a taxi for half the amount requested by the first taxi. Our accommodation was eight minutes away and the first taxi man could have rushed us there and back.

However, he preferred to sit and wait for non-existent customers, rather than be a businessman. Posada Enki did not disappoint. The self-contained rooms were very pleasant – single cabins with two rooms, a kitchen, and a toilet. They were built to accommodate four people. It also had a pool which was the perfect place for us to cool down after a long humid day. It was worth being there for the quiet and privacy. We met the owner and had a bit of a chat about our travels, and the day was done. Although the day had not begun on a positive note, we could not complain about the way it turned out.

Argentinian Side

28th March

We planned to wake up early and go to Iguazu Falls from the Argentinian side. We slept in and left our cabin at 9.00 a.m., walking one kilometre to a very small shopping centre where we bought some fruit from a man who was selling by the roadside. During the interaction, we asked him where we could get the bus to Iguzu City.

He pointed to the bus stop opposite his fruit cart. Argentinians drive on the right side of the road, and it takes some time for left-side drivers to fully get that into their heads. While we were sitting at the bus stop, we met a lady who was selling her goods from a pastry table. She started talking about something in Spanish, but we had no comprehension of what she was talking about. Then she mentioned 'travel' and 'bus', and with my little Spanish I told her that we were going to Iguazu city. She responded by saying the buses from that stop were not going to Iguazu but to somewhere different. She also said we had to walk to the main road to get the bus. With that, we bought two pastry scones from her, and walked three kilometres to the main road. On the main road, we sat on the wrong side of the road again. By the time we had realised that two buses had already left. We crossed the road and waited for buses to come – two passed by without stopping, even when we indicated that we were potential passengers. We got fed up waiting and took a taxi to the city. Once there we bought the tickets to visit Iguazu Falls from the Argentinian side.

We bought the entry tickets and took the small train to the Falls. There were two stops along the way, where people hopped on and off. There were also different trails to walk through. We went straight to the main trail and walked to the Falls. To see the Falls from this side revealed even more clearly how strong they were, and the mist rising from the water was refreshingly cool on our humidity - affected bodies. There were also places one could sit down, where butterflies and birds just hovered around. The butterflies landed on our bodies, and I noticed they were sucking our sweat. At first, I was not sure why, but I imagined it was due to the salt produced through the sweat. Overall, the Falls exceeded my expectations, no wonder they attracted tourists from all over the world. It was an unforgettable place.

Last days in Buenos Aires
29th and 30th March

Our Iguazu Falls trip came to an end, and we left for Buenos Aires. The traffic from the main city to Ezeiza was very congested. It took us two hours to get to our accommodation. Dinner was delicious in a cafe within Ezeiza shopping centre, and I could not believe it cost us only thirty Australian dollars including drinks. In Australia, it could have cost at least a hundred and fifty dollars including one drink each. This was our last day in Argentina, and we had nothing organised. We looked around Ezeiza, got some fruits and sat at a public park watching what was happening. The park was well maintained with few benches for people to sit on. We had dinner at the same hotel, but little did we know that one meal was enough for two people.

We were served a lot of food, ate as much as we could and left the rest, which made me feel terrible since I have a 'non-wastage of food policy'. I had ordered calamari and the plate was full. I have never seen such a serving of calamari for the very cheap price of nineteen Australian dollars. Afterwards, we went off to bed, waiting for the next day to fly out back to Australia.

GOING HOME

31st March

Our holiday was finished and it was time to go back to reality. As most people will know, it is difficult to sleep well on the final night. Our flight was at 7.10 a.m. and we had to be at the airport at 4.10 a.m. Valeria, our 'taxi lady', dropped us at the airport. Life is an interesting thing – sometimes you meet people and get along very well, even though you might never see them again in your whole life. Valeria was such a friend and an asset to us in Buenos Aires, and her hospitality was of a high standard.

We said our goodbyes, parted ways and left for Santiago. Our first flight to Santiago was with a Dutch airline. The flight was on time, and we received a very warm welcome. The staff was friendly, and the food was great. In Santiago, we went to the Qantas gate and, as always, they were not on time; it was something we expected. We waited and were finally ready to board for our destination. But just before we boarded the staff started searching for liquids over a hundred millilitres in volume. Who in this age does not know that it is a rule – you cannot carry on board over a hundred millilitres of liquid?

The guy who checked my bag racially profiled me; everyone else who went through was allowed to remove their wares from their bags. When it came to my turn, he warned me not to touch my bag or say anything. I thought that was unnecessary and never understood the point he was trying to make. Anyway, I just played dumb; he had his two seconds of power, and I could not care less. All I wanted was to board the plane back home. The Qantas staff on this flight seemed as though they did not want to be working. They were just going through the motions of their job.

Unlike the flight to Buenos Aires, where the food was good, the food on this flight was tired – soggy lettuce, for example – and they ran out of some items which they had indicated were available on the menu. There was a shortage of drinks and even water was barely offered. Sad to say, my friend had warned me about flying with Qantas, but there is little alternative when it comes to flying to South America from Australia. Lesson learnt! It will be a long time before I spend my money on them again, unless they changed their ways or there was no option.

We landed in Sydney, and I found the Immigration staff had no interest in welcoming their citizens back – or even in being hospitable to tourists. It was such a contrast to other countries I have travelled to; usually, Immigration staff are happy to welcome people back to their home country, or to wish tourists a pleasant stay. It felt as if we were bothersome to Immigration once we landed in Australia. Since my passport could not pass through the passport booths, I proceeded to the counter where I encountered a middle-aged Caucasian lady. Seeking to be pleasant, I proceeded to ask her 'how was your day?' She never responded, and I decided to be cheeky. So, I remarked that her day must have been horrible if she could not respond. She did not know what to do or say; all she did was ask for my passport.

I think by that time she had enough of me and stamped my declaration card with the quarantine assessment. I went through quarantine where the gentaleman was good in his manners and demeanour. He wanted to know what I had in my bag, and make sure that, as stated on the card I carried, I had nothing that would put Australia in danger. He was also interested in knowing where we had been, and the story of our Antarctica journey surprised him. We said goodbye and he let us exit to the domestic transfer. We had yet to fly on to Melbourne and of course, endure the now familiar delays with Qantas... Finally, we got back home to Melbourne, and the conclusion of the amazing, interesting story of our Antarctica trip.

Black-browed albatross

Relaxing in paradise

Mountains covered by glacier

The lazy seals

Jane N. Hughes

Curious of what was happening

M/V Ushuaia waiting for us

The whales took us by surprise

Jane N. Hughes

www.ingramcontent.com/pod-product-compliance
Lightning Source LLC
Chambersburg PA
CBHW040243010526
44107CB00065B/2860